101 SUPER SPORTS JOKES

by J.B. STAMPER

illustrated by Don Orehek

SCHOLASTIC INC.
New York Toronto London Auckland Sydney

ISBN 0-590-41435-6

22 21 20 19 18 17 16 15 14 13   3/9

Printed in the U.S.A.   01

First Scholastic printing, March 1988

CONTENTS

ALL-SPORTS SCRAMBLE

Why did the football coach send in his second string?

To tie up the game.

Why do soccer players have so much trouble eating popcorn balls?

They think they can't use their hands.

What do you get if you cross a karate
expert with a pig?

A pork chop.

Did you hear about the karate expert who joined the Army?

The first time he saluted, he cracked his helmet.

Why did the basketball wear a bib?

So it wouldn't dribble.

What do you call a boomerang that doesn't come back?

A stick.

Football Player: Coach, my doctor says I can't play football.
Coach: You didn't have to go to a doctor. I could have told you that.

Why do fast-food lovers do so well in marathons?

They like to eat and run.

How does a hockey player kiss?

He puckers up.

What do you get when you cross a
computer with a track-and-field star?

A floppy discus thrower.

Swimming Instructor: Remember, girls, swimming is the best exercise you can do to stay slim and beautiful.

Girl: Have you ever taken a close look at a duck?

What is a hermit?

A girl's baseball glove.

Who has played for every hockey team
in the National Hockey League?

*The organist at Madison Square
Garden.*

Why did the football player complain to the waiter?

There was a fly in his soup-er bowl.

What should a runner eat before a race?

Ketchup.

What was the nearsighted chicken doing on the baseball diamond?

Trying to hatch a fowl ball.

Reporter: How long have you been running?
Track Star: Since I was eight years old.
Reporter: Gee, you must be tired.

What do pigs do when they play
basketball?

Hog the ball.

What do you get if you cross a karate
expert with a tree?

Spruce Lee.

What do you get if you tie two bikes together?

Siamese Schwinns.

The ticket seller at a high school basketball game let in the chicken, the turkey, the pheasant, and the goose. But he turned away the duck. Why?

Five fowls and you're out.

A group of hikers were being led through the wilderness by a guide. On the third day, the hikers noticed that they had been traveling in circles.

"We're lost!" one hiker complained. "And you said you were the best guide in the United States."

"I am," the guide answered, "but I think we may have wandered into Canada."

Game Warden: Didn't you see the sign? It says, "No Fishing."
Boy: I'm not fishing. I'm teaching these worms how to swim.

HOME-RUN HUMOR

Why couldn't they sell soda pop at the doubleheader?

The home team lost the opener.

When does a baseball player wear armor?

To play the knight games.

Two baseball teams played a game.
One team won without a man
touching home base. How?

They were all-girl teams.

There was an umpire who was famous for wandering all over the baseball diamond. During one game, he got hit on the head by a foul ball and fell down.

The catcher said, "We've just witnessed the fall of the roamin' umpire."

Knock-knock.
Who's there?
Homer.
Homer who?
Homer flew right out of the ballpark.

First Boy: Wow! It's a run-home!
Second Boy: You mean a home run.
First Boy: No, I mean a run-home.
  You just hit the ball through the
  neighbor's window!

Little Leaguer: Dad, what does a ballplayer do when his eyesight starts going bad?
Dad: He gets a job as an umpire.

Where is the headquarters of the Umpires' Association?

The Umpire State Building.

Why does a baseball pitcher raise one leg when he pitches?

If he raised both legs, he would fall down.

For homework the teacher asked her students to make a list of nine great Americans. The next day, everyone handed in their papers except Bobby.

"Bobby, couldn't you finish the assignment?" the teacher asked.

"I got eight of them," Bobby answered. "But I just couldn't decide on the second baseman."

Why was the new shortstop like
Cinderella?

He ran away from the ball.

How should a girl flirt with a baseball
player?

Bat her eyelashes.

Little-League Vampire: Dad, what's the best way to hold a bat?
Father Vampire: By the wings, son.

Why does it take longer to run from second base to third base than it takes to run from first base to second base?

Because there's a shortstop between second and third.

What is chocolate and is in the Baseball Hall of Fame?

Babe Ruth.

Little Brother: Thanks for the baseball cards, but I can't read yet.
Big Brother: Don't worry. You can still look at the pitchers.

What do you get if you cross a lizard with a baseball player?

An outfielder who catches flies with his tongue.

Knock-knock.
Who's there?
Philip.
Philip who?
Philip the bases.

Knock-knock.
Who's there?
Uriah.
Uriah who?
Keep Uriah on the ball.

Knock-knock.

Who's there?

José.

José who?

José, can you see by the dawn's early light. . . .

It was the new pitcher's first game on the mound, and he was not having a good day. After walking his third straight player, the manager came out for a talk.

"That's enough," the manager said. "It's time I bring in a relief pitcher."

"But look who's up to bat," the pitcher said. "Last time that guy was up, I struck him out."

"Yeah, I know," the manager said. "But this is still the same inning."

Where should a baseball team never wear red?

In the bullpen.

Doctor: What happened to you?
Patient: I went camping with a baseball player.
Doctor: What's that got to do with your black eye?
Patient: I told him to pitch the tent, and he did.

What do you call a player who falls
asleep in the bullpen?

A bulldozer.

What has eighteen legs and catches
flies?

A baseball team.

FOOTBALL FUNNIES

What is a pigskin for?

To hold a pig together.

Definition of a Coach: Someone who is willing to lay down your life for the school.

How is an airline pilot like a football player?

They both like to make safe touchdowns.

What should a fullback do when he gets a handoff?

Go to a secondhand store.

What do you call the football player who guesses the other team's plays?

The hunchback.

Knock-knock.
Who's there?
Justin.
Justin who?
Justin time for the kickoff.

Knock-knock.
Who's there?
Ice cream.
Ice cream who?
Ice cream 'cause I'm a cheerleader.

Boy: Doc, do you think I can play
football after this cast is off my leg?
Doctor: Certainly.
Boy: Thanks. I couldn't play before.

Why did the football player do a
commercial for hair shampoo?

He was troubled by split ends.

What's green, has bumps, and plays football?

The Green Bay Pickles.

Dad: How'd you do in the game today, son?

Son: I made a ninety-two yard run.

Dad: That's terrific!

Son: Not really. I didn't catch the guy I was chasing.

What's black and white and sticky all over?

A referee who fell into the Sugar Bowl.

What is a cheerleader's favorite drink?

Root beer.

What is a cheerleader's favorite color?

Yeller.

What's black and white and green all over?

A referee who fell into the Gator Bowl.

Only thirteen seconds were left in the fourth quarter of a big football game. The home team was ahead by three points and had possession of the ball. The quarterback threw a pass to a first-year player, who caught it, then dropped it. The opposing team recovered the ball and went on to score the winning touchdown.

Asked how he felt about the defeat, the home team's coach said, "Well, that's how the rookie fumbles."

Why did the ghost try out for the cheerleading squad?

To add a little team spirit.

Jack: How did you break your arm?

Zack: I was playing football with a telephone booth.

Jack: What?

Zack: I was trying to get my quarter back!

SPORTS
BEST-SELLERS

Strike Three
by
U.R. Out

Last-Inning Cliffhangers
by
D. Bases   R. Loaded

Last-Second Touchdown
by
Justin Time

Interception
by
E. Bluitt

The Referee Is Always Right
by
R.U. Nuts

Sports Medicine
by
Frank N. Stein

The Washington Redskins
by
T.P. Dweller

Great Basketball Plays
by
Jim Shoes

Improve Your Foul Shooting
by
Mr. Completely

OUT-OF-BOUNDS BASKETBALL

Why does it get hot after a basketball game?

Because all the fans have gone.

Why was Cinderella such an awful basketball player?

She had a pumpkin for a coach.

How do they play basketball in
Hawaii?

With Hula Hoops.

Basketball Coach: Billy, I think you grew another foot over the summer.
Billy: No, Coach, honest. I still have only two.

Why did the bench-sitter bring a water pistol to the basketball game?

He wanted a chance to shoot the ball.

Why did the retired basketball player become a judge?

To stay on the court.

What is Wilt the Stilt's middle name?

The.

Reporter: Do you like all of your players to be tall, Coach?

Famous Coach: A player's height isn't important to me, as long as his ears pop when he sits down.

What disease makes you a better basketball player?

Athlete's foot.

What dessert should basketball players never eat?

Turnovers.

What team is known for traveling
with the ball?

The Harlem Globe-Trotters.

What do you get if you cross a
basketball player with a groundhog?

*Six more weeks of the basketball
season.*

Why was the basketball player
holding his nose?

Someone was taking a foul shot.

Reporter: What's the hardest thing you have to do every day?
Famous Basketball Star: Tie my shoes.

What is a personal foul?

Your very own chicken.

MORE SPORTS BEST-SELLERS

Basketball Bloopers
by
Dub L. Dribble

Calisthenics
by
Stan Dupp and Neil Down

Skateboard Hotdogging
by
Frank Furter

Ice Hockey for Beginners
by
I.M. Freezin

Hockey Plays
by
I.C. Tose

Bowling Strikes
by
M.T. Lane

Boxing Knockouts
by
Seymour Stars

SOCCER LAUGHS

What's the best place to shop for a soccer shirt?

New Jersey.

What were the soccer star's first words as a baby?

Look, Ma, no hands.

Father: What did you think of your first soccer game, son?

Son: It was okay, Dad, but those guys never learned how to share.

Father: Why do you say that?

Son: They're still fighting over who gets the ball.

What position did the monster play on the soccer team?

Ghoulie.

First Fan: I can tell you what the score's going to be before this game starts.

Second Fan: Really, what is it?

First Fan: Nothing to nothing.

Knock-knock.
Who's there?
Ooze.
Ooze who?
Ooze got the ball?

Knock-knock.
Who's there?
Soccer.
Soccer who?
Soccerjawea.

Teacher: Johnny, name the four
  seasons.
Johnny: Football, basketball,
  baseball, and soccer.

First Fan: What's the score of the game?

Second Fan: Eight to five.

First Fan: Who's winning?

Second Fan: Eight.

Angry Man: Little boy, have you seen who broke my window?

Little Boy: No, but have you seen my soccer ball?

SILLY SPORTS TALK

"Looks like I missed the bull's-eye,"
Tom said aimlessly.

"Give me a rubdown," Tom said sorely.

"Let's go camping if the weather is
good," Tom said tentatively.

"I've got a great tennis serve," Tom said faultlessly.

"Would you go fishing with me?" Tom asked with baited breath.

"What this team needs is a great home-run hitter," Tom said ruthlessly.

"I'm retiring from baseball," Tom said with resignation.

"Something is wrong with my bowling," Tom said gutterally.

"Is this boat tilting, or is it my imagination?" Tom asked listlessly.

"Want to Indian wrestle?" Tom asked bravely.

"Our canoe is headed for the falls!" Tom said rapidly.

"This horse won't stop," Tom said woefully.

WRESTLING RIOT

What are a wrestler's favorite colors?

Black and blue.

First Wrestler: I've got you in a
scissors hold.
Second Wrestler: Cut it out!

First Wrestler: Want to see something really swell?
Second Wrestler: Sure.
First Wrestler: Hit yourself on the head with a baseball bat.

First Wrestler: I hear you're taking a mail-order bodybuilding course.

Second Wrestler: That's right. Every week, the mailman brings me a new piece of bodybuilding equipment.

First Wrestler: You don't look much different to me.

Second Wrestler: You're right. But you should see my mailman!

Why did the wrestlers have to wrestle in the dark?

Their match wouldn't light.

First Wrestler: That sure was a long walk from the dressing room to the ring.
Second Wrestler: Don't worry. You won't have to walk back.

First Fan: Did you hear about the wrestler whose nose ran and feet smelled?

Second Fan: No, what was wrong with him?

First Fan: He was built upside down.

First Fan: Did you see the match
  between Frankenstein and Dracula?
Second Fan: No. What happened?
First Fan: Frankenstein was down
  for the Count.

First Wrestler: How would you like a knuckle sandwich?

Second Wrestler: No, thanks. I'm a vegetarian.

Manager: How did you ever get out of that hold?

Wrestler: It happened like this: I saw a finger, so I bit it. Then I got really mad 'cause my finger hurt so bad!

Manager: Can you join me in a cup of coffee?

Wrestler: Think we'll both fit?

Why are wrestlers so good at geometry?

Because they're used to circling in a square ring.